Dedication

I dedicate Bittersweet to both my Auntie Harriet and my young cousin Malaika. Malaika has been living with type 1 diabetes for coming up to six years and was diagnosed on April 24th, 2016, at just six years old. Malaika turns 12 years old on January 11th, which will mark 100 years since the first human being, Leonard Thompson, was administered the first injection of insulin. It is also the release day of Bittersweet. Happy Birthday Malaika!

I will always remember the awesome and supportive conversation and advice that you gave to me Malaika, when I was first diagnosed. You and your Mum are both so resilient and strong, but not scared to show your emotions, which I find courageous. What you go through every day, shows how powerful you really are! Your support means so much to me. Keep being you, the type 1 warrior you are! With love, Duke.

Contents Page

Duke Al

Bitter Sweet

- - - - - - - - - - - -

The Highs, The Lows, Hypers and
Hypos of Living with Type 1 Diabetes

Artwork by Sarah Racanière

Published by Amazon KDP

Foreword

Hello readers!

I first met Duke 10,160 days ago today; today being the 5th January 2022. To save you searching for an abacus or trying to strain your brain from something I could simply explain, I can tell you that that was the day Duke Al Durham was born. I am Duke's older (and of course the more handsome) brother. Pardon my attempt at writing poetry or as some might say - a rhyme? Well, that's what I always thought poetry was. Or, that in order for a series of words to constitute as a poem, the only criteria is that it must rhyme.

I suppose that's probably what a lot of people understand poetry to be – a clever rhyme - but I can assure you from understanding my brother more and more over the years, poetry is so much more than that. In my eyes Duke is a genius - his ability to express himself with words continues to astound me and I find myself, more than anything, marvelling at his courage, resilience, and determination.

Growing up, Duke was always the "sporty one" and I was the "creative one." I started playing the trombone when I was eight years old and what was my vocation has turned into my daily bread. I love it. Music is my passion, and I was sure that sport, was Duke's. He was visibly naturally gifted at it. He was good at football. He played rugby for his school, local club, local county and was picked for Cardiff Blues development squad. He is strong, quick, and fearless. He competed at track and field events as part of his local athletics club including the one hundred metres, two hundred metres, four and eight hundred metres, long jump, triple jump, high jump -to name a few. He pursued a degree in Sports Coaching and became a personal trainer and I'd also like to mention that he has been an auxiliary firefighter for seven and a half years too.

On the surface, Duke seemed happy with what he was doing, however, unbeknown to me for years, he was in fact struggling. Trying to cope with intrusive thoughts and compulsions. He was diagnosed with Obsessive Compulsive Disorder (OCD) at sixteen years old.

From around the age of eleven Duke started listening to rap artists and I believe this was the start of his poetry (and music) journey. He would learn raps off by heart and practise in his bedroom and you could tell he enjoyed it because our neighbours would knock on our door and ask if he could turn down the music! He was inspired and we noticed he started writing his own raps. The content was, somewhat questionable, at first (think along the lines of early Jay – Z, Eminem, 50 Cent, Dr. Dre etc) but Duke later began writing about his own thoughts and how he was feeling. He was passionate; he had A4 paper pads filled with raps, poems...thoughts. It was his escapism, his liberation.

I arrived back at Heathrow on the 21st of January 2018 after working with the Scottish National Ballet in Aberdeen performing The Nutcracker. I was waiting for my coach to take me back home and my mum rang. She asked if I had arrived safely, and the usual things mums ask when you've been away for more than a day. The conversation had come to a natural end and then mums tone changed. She told me that Duke had been diagnosed with type 1 diabetes. I felt my eyes overflow with tears, and I wept uncontrollably.

I think the reason I was so unbelievably upset wasn't solely because of the new diagnosis but because I had witnessed my brother fighting an exhausting, mental disability first-hand for over ten years and I know what he has been through; and now this. At the time, I remember wishing it was me instead of him.

I am incredibly proud of my brother, and it gives me immense joy and pleasure to write this foreword. In the face of adversity and despite the challenges he has faced over the years, he has always remained strong-willed and maintained his integrity and character throughout. His OCD and his type 1 diabetes is part of him. He has learnt to live with it and not against it, producing a brilliant by-product which fuels his mind to write poems.

I am always intrigued what the next poem is going to be, or indeed what his next venture will be. Duke writes purely from his heart and soul, every word he has experienced, and I have no doubt that you will find these poems powerful, insightful, and often profound.

Duke gives a voice to those who are unable to find the right words, and inspires those who can, to speak louder.

To you, the reader, I thank you for your support and hope this book has an impact on you however great or small.

To you, my brother, I love you.
Jake Durham

INTRODUCTION

Invincible

What are your superpowers?

When I was a kid, I had my tonsils removed. Before surgery I remember talking to my Mum as she held my hand. I was given a general anaesthetic, it was meant to make me fall asleep, as I laid there wide awake, I heard the doctors say 'wow this boy's strong', I mean a lot of kids around the world probably reacted the same way to general anaesthetic, but at that moment I felt unique, unstoppable. I was quickly given another dose and I was asleep. When I awoke, my Mum reminded me of the story, I smiled in disbelief, I knew I was invincible.

My fascination with superheroes began even younger, I used to wear the Spider-Man suit my Mum bought me, everywhere! I'd put it on when walking to the shops down the road and it instantly made me feel invincible. Ever since the Incredible Hulk burst onto the TV, he has been my favourite superhero, an indestructible force that can destroy any enemy, overcome any obstacle and never have fear.

I was always strong willed growing up, giving up was never an option. I wanted to prove to myself and everybody around me how capable I was at sport, how much talent I knew I had flowing through my veins, how much drive I had to succeed. A determination to never stay down and always get back up, a sheer will to be invincible.

At around 13 years old I began experiencing horrifying intrusive thoughts, such as family members dying. I felt an unstoppable urge to pray repetitively. I thought it was my responsibility to do so, a compulsion, otherwise the intrusive thought could happen, and it would be my fault. The lives of family members were burdened on my shoulders, the uncertainty of whether I prayed enough times, or correctly said the prayers with no mistakes to prevent the intrusive thoughts from happening, swallowed me. I was lost, in a vicious cycle of what I soon found out to be Obsessive Compulsive Disorder (OCD). My kryptonite. My weakness to the superhero persona I always wanted.

Along came alcohol, in the form of a quick fix drink, a coping mechanism. I became a weekend binge drinker from the age of 14. A user and abuser, I would try to hide the amount I drank from my Mum, when I was able to get my hands-on alcohol with my mates. I found myself on the weekends drunk, paralytic, a mess. It became a problem, it became my second weakness to my superhero persona, another barrier stopping me from being invincible.

I eventually got the help I needed in early adulthood, after throwing myself in front of a car, under the influence of alcohol, yet at the mercy of OCD. I just had enough of the relentless torture, the taunts from OCD, the fear of something bad happening, the responsibility, the uncertainty, the stress, the anxiety in my stomach to my chest, to the edge of my fingertips and toes, I had enough of the noise. I was hit. All I had wrong with me after smashing the windscreen of the car and falling, face first, off the bonnet onto the concrete road, was a cut and a bruise on my face.

Invincible?
Maybe.
Lucky?
Definitely.

The day I finally realised that I was not invincible, was January the 18th 2018 when I was diagnosed with type 1 diabetes. The sport I used to compete in, the physical talent I had, the physique I could get myself into when going to the gym, it all felt lost. It all felt as though I could never reach my full potential ever again. I could never be the superhero I wanted to be when I was young. My newly found condition, another weakness. How could I be the best and strongest version of myself, if I had to rely on insulin every single day for the rest of my life, to keep me alive, let alone manage my OCD. I have asked myself that question over and over again. I struggled with various difficulties after my diagnosis, which are represented within Bittersweet.

I am the type of person who believes everything happens for a reason. I believe that I was meant to get type 1 diabetes, even if it was just to write Bittersweet. To reach out to others who are living with the relentless condition, to relate to them so they do not feel alone and help educate others who do not understand the condition. For myself to recognise that what I am going through with OCD and T1D and what I have been through with alcohol, takes resilience, it takes courage, takes strength to overcome every single day and still continue to smile. Now, if they are not superhero traits, I don't know what are!

Please do not see this as narcissism, as it really could not be further from it. It has taken me ages to learn to live with my imperfections, they are a part of me. I think we need to give ourselves a little break and a tap on the back sometimes because we are superheroes, we are our own superheroes, saving our own lives every day.

I believe in this life, we have a choice in every situation we are faced with. It is up to us to make a decision. We will continue to manage our daily challenge of balance. We will have highs, lows, hypers and hypos but we will never give in. When our spirits are lifted after this life on Earth to begin our next journey, we will know that we may have imperfections in our vehicles that we ride on Earth, yet our spirits can never be broken. Our souls are perfection because deep down, deep within, running through our electric spinal cords, with energy tingling towards our fingertips, we have the superpowers to do anything, we are invincible.

My Story

T1D

My Story - T1D

I put the cartridge ink in the pen and write about how I am
affected,
Then I put the insulin in the pen and slowly inject it,
Ironic, a poetic diabetic.

This may sound funny, I get it,
Yet, these last few years have been hectic,
Running high in flight for so long, then suddenly I skydived
plummeted,
Luckily my parachute ejected.

My pancreas decided to give up, triggered by a Salmonella
bug which turned septic,
A bacterial disease I caught in Bali near the Monkey Forest,
Along with things that I was stressed with,
Dealing with OCD, PTSD and stress of my final year of
university,
Others behind my back calling me lazy.
Mouth dry, constantly thirsty,
As I put the liquid to my lips,
I could not help but drink and drink,
Not realising I was like a sieve,
As I urinated and urinated the sugar,
My body could not live with.

Diagnosed at 23 type 1 diabetes.

I had wondered why my energy, had felt so low,
I suppose it was the glucose, those symptoms of lethargy.
Hyperglycemia that I thought was just feelings of adulthood,
All of that sugar that my body could not absorb, floating
around in my blood.
How tired I always was, I mean extremely lethargic,
No pump in the gym even when I worked out my hardest!
The strangest feeling,
I began to lose weight, I never had the faintest idea why

At first I got along with my new lifestyle,
I swerved the wrong foods, started eating to preserve my
lifestyle,
I got used to the daily injections and blood testing,
Just one month later I found myself protesting, objection,
Huge frustration of my newly found diagnosis came with
rejection,
I was angry, I felt I could not compete as well as I used to
when I played rugby,
Am I weak?
The next stage after rage was neglect,
I suffer with OCD and it told me not to inject,
Consuming scary amounts of alcohol was my downward
fall,

Because I never knew the potentially fatal effects.
I was battling mental health and diabetes something had to intercept,
Before I destroyed my body, in debt,
As I was taking time away from my life,
A year later I knew I'd pay the price,
If I kept allowing myself, my health to self-destruct,
So, I picked back up the pen to reconstruct,
I wrote about how I felt, emotion out on the page, it was enough,
I got help, went on the DAFNE course, yet days still can be tough.
But I am happy I am here living with T1D,
It will never get the better of me,
I would like to thank Sir Frederick G. Banting who discovered Insulin,
As without him I would not be here living.

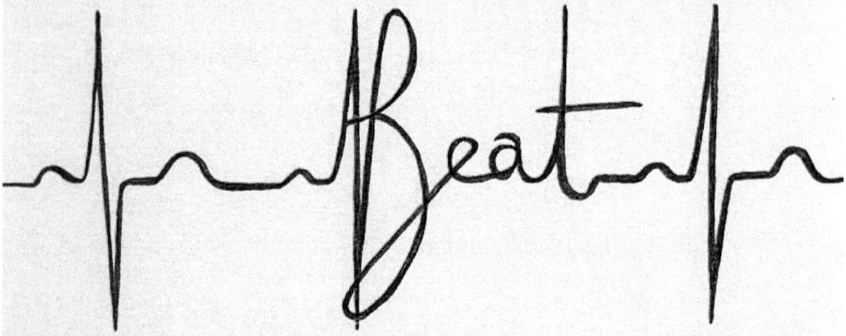
Beat

Beat

My heart beats,
My pulse beats,
A rhythm within me that sparks these,
Ideas, large dreams,
A belief, a path seen,
A journey, with a purpose,
If I was heartless I'd be worthless.
I was meant to have to fight,
To make a choice in my life,
Whether to be beaten, left to die,
Or stand back up, willing to do more than survive,
I was meant to write poetry,
To perform, to connect, I know it's me,
It's my calling, these words I speak,
To relate and educate, bringing comfort, understanding and peace,
To those who need it most,
To those who feel it close,
In their beating hearts in which they hold,
Who used to be ghosts, lost souls,
But now, do not feel alone.
I believe we all have a purpose on this planet,
We all have gifts and talents,
Find yours, it will naturally beat,

We are all unique.

My blood flows,
Off-beat,
Yet type 1 diabetes,
Will never beat me.

Box of Chocolates

If life is like a box of chocolates,
And you never know what you're gonna get, it's pot luck
Would our chocolate,
Be boxed-up,
In an Amazon truck,
Stocked up,
To the top,
Topped up,
With extra sugar ready to fight a monster of a hypo?
You know, that first ever hypo that knocked us,
Never stopped us,
But really knocked us.
Or is it a bittersweet metaphor?

Hidden Hypos

I hide my hypos.
I don't want to be seen behind closed doors,
As the guy who always falls so low,
Who 'skives' from work, until he feels right so...

I disguise my hypos.
I focus deeply when in a convo,
As I subtly eat Dextrose,
Waiting for the glucose to reload,
I don't want the person to know,
Or think I'm uninterested so...

I hide my hypos,
By acting.
I keep control of my cravings,
I pretend I'm fine,
Then leave the room silently, inside shaking.
It makes me feel weak, I want to be seen as strong so...

I disguise my hypos,
When at the gym,
I just say I'm tired and need a drink,
Wait for the sugar to kick in,
People assume I'm just unfit so...

I hide my hypos,
From judgemental individuals,
Who would say something like...
Oh, he's hypoing again,
Must not have good control,
Roll their eyes,
Think they understand, assume I'm reckless, won't listen,
To the Doctors advice I've been given.
So, I keep it hidden.
It's embarrassing,
Not worth the criticism.

I used to be hyper when I was younger,
Energy formed within.
Now hyper means something completely different,
I'm lucky I'm still living in the Honeymoon period,
I can feel myself getting real low, in a sticky situation.
Although it can catch me with a sting, a hypo that's tricky to
hide in conversation.

As inside I wanna go psycho, hulk out, destroy everything!
Body in fight or flight mode, craving the sugar my body
cannot bin,
Ironic,

I guess I injected too much insulin...
Or didn't account for the caffeine, the burpees or the Sun's heat,
I hide my hypos, force Mr. Hyde to stay within.

But now you better hide and give me food,
This hypo's uncontrollable, I don't mean to be rude,
But I'm in a survival instinct mood!
I'm hangry.

Sugar Coated

Go on just have another drink,
Diabetes *probably* is not as bad as you think,
It's not like you have work in the morning,
Come on one more won't hurt, don't be boring,
You can run high for one night,
Forget injecting, you're here to have fun, right?
What? Are you tongue tied?
Please don't say no, I thought you were a fun guy?
Please know, this is not peer pressure,
I want you to know more people are worse off than you.
So, what do you fear Trevor?
Don't let insulin rule you forever,
Just one night of pleasure,
Let's have a few more drinks together.

The Forgotten Appointment

How has your control been lately?
Have you done your bloods for your HbA1c?
Have you had your eye screening?
Your feet, do they still have feeling?
Do you wear the freestyle Libre?
Can I check your average on your glucose meter?
Perhaps you could think about a pump?
Has your dentist checked out your gums?
Have you completed a DAFNE course?
Do you adjust your insulin before you play sport?
Do you need help with anything else?

'Yes, what about my mental health?
I know everything may seem hunky dory,
But my body and mind tell a different story.'

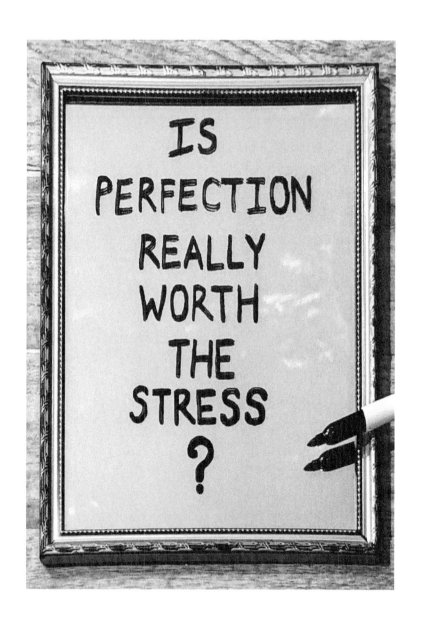

Perfect

I try to be perfect in every aspect of my life,
I try not to hurt anybody's feelings or let them down,
I try to show empathy when listening to those who are so
low that the ground-
Feels above them,
That their only way out, is a tiny hole of light that seems
impossible to squeeze through,
I try to give people advice and hope.

I try to be a good person in every aspect of my life,
I try and help others,
But then I neglect myself.
I strive for perfection through others, ensuring I am making
them happy,
But what about my health?

I say yes to so many it has turned habitual,
I perform daily rituals to wipe out imperfections.
My blood glucose is never perfect,
I want to help others, but I need self-reflection.

Is perfection really worth the stress?
I want perfect control I really do.
Should I put myself first?

Maybe...
Perfect control is not realistic,
When I concentrate,
I am in target range often,
But it's not perfect and it probably will never be,
Just like other aspects of my life.

Trying to be perfect is like walking on a bridge of glass, with
metal spiked shoes.
As long as there is a conscious will, to do what is right to
look after yourself,
The energy and effort to do so will follow,
Perfection is not worth stressing over,
As imperfection makes us human,
I try to do my best and that is what makes me happy.

Candle

Scratch the smooth match, across the rough patch, fast,
Light the candle stick and watch as the wax drips, drips...
Then burns out.

It's funny how things turn out,
One minute optimistic, a full candle stick,
The next a molten mess, melted miserably,
By conflicted emotions, exhaustion.
It's not like we could see it coming to this.
Candle sticks are all different sizes.
As time diminishes, until the flame finishes,
We keep our light.

The half-way point can be an indication of feeling tiresome,
With each drop of wax we lose,
We find some energy deep within, to keep us burning.
Each sharp sting to the skin,
All the countless counting,
It starts to sink in.
Inside we are shouting,
Then we stumble, as the candle gets weaker,
We shake at the knees, a wobble that features,
Lower than lows, our eyes heavy, breathing deeper.

Highs and lows, the candle bleak, as wax falls,
Struggling to handle the balance,
To get hold of the impossible angle,
Of control.

We strangle ourselves with frustration,
Others think it's a common UK moan,
We look for help as the flame burns out.
But who will understand, who can resonate?
We feel alone.
A lost candle loathing in the dark,
Wondering how to reignite its spark.

It's funny how life turns out,
One minute optimistic, the next, fatigued, a mess, over stressed,
A condition of relentless tests.
No wonder we hit burnout,
But we are doing our best...

It Cannot Be

Please,
This cannot be,
My son's face is confused,
As he stares at me,
His eyes are glazed,
I prick his finger, he's brave,
But the noise draws fear to his face,
A small sharp pain,
That saddens me.

A tiny bit of blood, on the tip of his tiny finger,
It's thicker than mine it's brighter, it's richer,
I know how it feels, when the lancet is loaded,
Then fired, blood appears, tiny nerve sensors have
exploded.
Lately he's been unusually thirsty,
With dark shadows under his eyes,
Going to the toilet more than usual,
He's only five,
It cannot be...

My belly is hollow, empty doing flips,
Worry dries my throat, I cannot speak,
Like my tongue has twist,

I bite my lip,
I cannot show my son how I really feel,
I control my expressions, I smile, I kneel,
I comfort him,
We wait for the reading,
As my son says,
'Daddy, my fingers stopped bleeding',
I smile a little more, he doesn't understand,
5 seconds feels like a lifetime,
I hold his hand,
It cannot be...

Fears swim through my bloodstream,
I don't want to look, I cannot see...
I don't want my son to suffer from type 1,
Like me.

The Human Pancreas

The Human Pancreas is military,
Breakfast, Dinner, Tea, repeat,
A routine to monitor the blood, the carbs,
No day is easy, adjusting is hard.
A strict regime, it has to be,
The Human Pancreas is an emotional masterpiece,
Made up of strength, courage, but most of all, of love,
The Human Pancreas carefully pricks fingers, extracts
blood.
Every hour, delicate decisions are made,
The Human Pancreas gives insulin after food is weighed,
A Human calculator, a carbohydrate counting genius,
Armed with treats as treatment, so the sugar release is
immediate.
The Human Pancreas knows best,
Knows how, when, where and what to check and test,
Self-educating- knowledge is power,
A teacher, an understanding warrior,
A protector of their own warrior,
A worrier,
But that's Human nature.
A lifesaver, yearly, monthly, daily,
The Human Pancreas is a superhero to their child, to their
baby.

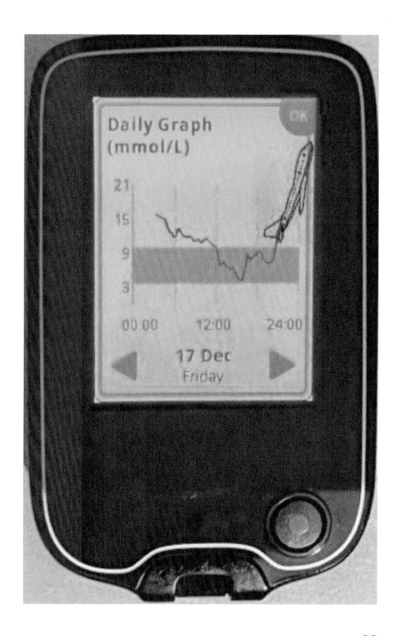

Luggage

I neglect insulin to punish myself.
I rummage through overflowing luggage my mind is
burdened with,
To figure out why self-doubt is weighing me down.
If I could at least close the suitcase,
Or throw away some clothes to lighten the load.
That feeling of having to punish myself, will it go away?

My blood sugar goes high,
I reject healthy foods,
Punishing must be encouraging to unhealthy eating,
I must avoid any nourishing vitamins and minerals,
My body cannot be flourishing.
I must feel pain, or at least the effects of hyperglycaemia.

I discourage myself,
Until I eventually lighten the overflowing luggage,
Somehow, I find the strength and the courage to offload the
weight,
I write as my escape, my break to break away, I look after
myself,
Until the following day,
An unpredictable cycle,
The luggage is overflowing again.

Welcome to the effects of mental health, of OCD and low self-esteem,
When living with an autoimmune condition.
My mind is jam packed,
My blood sugar is flying high,
Ironic, as I could do with a holiday.

Complications

My eyesight is not as good as it was,
Sometimes my toes go numb,
My biggest worry is glaucoma,
Or amputated feet, because I have type 1,
I know it's down to control,
But I still worry about diabetic comas,
If I have a bad night on alcohol,
At least I'm an organ donor,
But are my organs healthy enough?
Or are they slowly deteriorating?
My liver, a soldier, I'm sober,
My kidneys help with urinating,
Overworked, overloaded,
Running this machine can be a struggle,
But they're serving me well, nothing has yet exploded,
Am I waiting for something to burst my bubble?

Being in a hyper for so long,
How many hours have I shaved off my life?
It could be zero, I could be wrong,
It could days... At night,
My legs ache after drinking,
I'm so tired after a hypo,
It gets my mind overthinking,

I lose concentration, **typos**,
Are more likely when **riting**,
But I must stay optimistic,
A worried mindset is frightening,
Lyrics I write keep my spirits uplifted.

Mood Shots

I load up the barrel, I prepare to shoot,
Speech is slurred, breath stinks of booze,
I load up the shots, overthinking's my excuse,
I use and abuse, I'm not confused, I'm a loose
Cannon...
I've seen Hamilton,
Feel like I've blown my shot,
A mixture of conditions, will I spew? I hope not,
I'm hopeless my hope rots,
I am not throwing away my shots.

Pointe

Is a balance with such beauty hard to sustain?
Or once gained, easier to maintain?
Is it achievable to dance in life without worry?
Falling off balance in no hurry to change.

What's the point?
If it all falls down
What's the point?
If rebalance is not around
What's the point?
When all we do is hit the ground
What's the point?
Can you tell me now?

Astonishingly agile,
Beautifully balanced,
Continuously challenged.
Dangerously delicate,
Exquisitely elegant,
Frighteningly fragile.

On the very edge of the tiptoes,
Where posture is perfect, imbalance is challenged.
Just one wobble could cause a slip, so,

Concentration and consistency need to be well managed.

A balance with such beauty is hard to sustain,
The pointe of a ballet dancer to dance without pain,
Find the balance, once gained, they effortlessly keep shape,
Yet a balance with such beauty is hard to sustain.

On the very edge of euphoria and dystopia,
Directly in between, high and low,
Flows an Aurora of a warrior,
Touching the sky with a glow.

A balance with such beauty is hard to sustain,
What is the point if it can't be maintained?
But is that not the goal, the indefinite aim?
A balance with such beauty is hard to sustain.

But it is possible if we can change,
Parts of our lives which we know affect our range,
Educate our minds when the glucose feels untamed,
Live a lifestyle that will keep us dancing on stage,

The pointe is to find balance,
That is our life's challenge.

Description of A Hypo

It's not easy to describe how I feel when having a hypo,
Internally I often feel erratic,
My behaviour is impulsive, desperate,
I don't care about consequences,
I focus on re-energising,
By any means necessary.

Externally, I try to keep my composure,
As a mixture of feeling drunk and weak combines.
I try to ensure I'm still polite to people,
As my eyes begin to divide their focus,
I'm exhausted,
I'm nauseous,
I'm ravenous,
I eat-
I eat-
I eat-
And I keep on eating.

The feeling of *'normal'* is lagging slowly,
Dragging itself behind the enormous amount of carbs I
consume,
I try to stop,
But my body craves food.

20 minutes later I feel *'normal'*,
Yet fatigue and exhaustion last for 20 hours more.

How would you describe a hypo in the way it affects your mind and body?

Travelling Afar Could Be Painful

It's a pain carrying medication for long trips away,
But it's more painful forgetting it...

Burnt Out

I just don't know what to do anymore,
Taking my blood is such an exhausting chore,
I don't know whether to punch these four walls,
Or let gravity absorb me, push me, force me to fall towards
the Earth's core.
I am low... for once it's not a hypo low it's...
Because I've had it to the core with all of this,
The finger pricks, the tiny stings,
Sore fingertips from the small, yet continuous pain,
It's such a hindrance to my day.
I don't mean to complain,
My brain has just had enough,
I gain,
Nothing it seems from injecting,
I check my sugars, yet again they're high and need
correcting,
You know what,
I don't care this is wearing, insulin, I am neglecting,
Digesting anything I want, whenever I want to,
I think I've done enough of accepting my condition,
Expecting my sugars to be in range, no recognition,
For putting up with this every day.
Come on Pancreas give me a break,
I'm getting restless,

I need to take a moment to taste-
How it used to feel, to be able to eat a carbohydrate loaded
meal,
Without the stress...

2 Years

A few years...?
No.
I heard somewhere, just 2 years, a person could live without insulin.

That's 2 years,
People with T1D lived in true fears,
As it worsened every day, until they reached DKA and their body melted away.
2 years, on a starvation diet,
The body gets tired quick, appearance stick thin, sick,
Quietly, sudden and quick the inevitable, wreaks havoc,
The blood sugar, on a dangerous level causes conflict,
Riots inside the energy supply, mouth dry.

But we live in a time where artificial insulin saves our lives,
Those 2 years have become renewed years,
Those 2 years have become millions of years,
To laugh, to live, to be with the people we love,
To experience life in all of its wonder,
To look beyond the pondered,
As once upon a time,
As we wander, as I rhyme,
2 years would pass us by,
And we would not survive.

I will not waste a moment,
In this new life, I have been gifted.

Our Superpowers

True resilience
The ability to stand
Even when we fall

True self-awareness
To recognise when life's tough
And reach out for help

Relentless courage
To manage daily struggles
No matter the pain

A heart full of love
Bonded by experience
Stronger together

Unstoppable strength
We self-medicate hypos
When we're feeling weak

The Type 1 Warrior!

Every young Type 1 Warrior, has the ability to make magic!
The insulin pen is not just a pen, it's a wand to create
fantastic-
Things that stem, from the spectacular imagination,
The thoughts of a Type 1 Warrior are full of colours, wonder
and creation.
When deep into their dreams, they gain the power to create,
Anything they want, they hold the key, they wear the
warrior's cape.
They fight off all the baddies and of course they can fly,
As they use their magic pen, to make their toys come alive.
They help other people too, who need some uplifting,
They can run faster than any animal, jump high and love to
sing,
They are the strongest of all around, a strength formed
within,
For they are Type 1 Warriors, who have skills, inject insulin,
Accepted their condition, it's made them brave, never give
in,
Fight off all of the sugar, where in the blood it loves to
swim,
As nothing will ever stop them, from saving the planet
they're in,

For they are Type 1 Warriors, with a pen that creates magic things!

The Sugar Coater

Andy- John mate, you've only been in this job a year, yet
you've managed to break sales records with the fastest pay
rise I have ever seen in this company. So, I'm raising a glass
to your rise my friend, just as soon as I've bought us
another beer... actually are you alright to have another I
forget you're a diabetic?

John- Noo Andy, it's only diabetes, I'm fine,
I can have a few more pints.

Andy- Are you sure? I don't want you to spew all night,
Or have a wobbly on me.

John- Very funny, chill, as I said it's fine,
It's only diabetes, there's far more people worse off in life.

Andy- What does having diabetes mean for you anyway?

John- Oh it's nothing,
It's just, I don't want to make a scene,
It's an inconvenience I have to live with every day.

Andy- Can you elaborate and explain?
You say your sugars can go high, does it elevate your mood?

Or give you so much crazy energy you can literally levitate, lift the roof?

John- Woh, so many questions man, I'm a bit tipsy mate, I can barely concentrate!

Andy- Or are you dodging the question?
Look mate, I don't mean to interrogate but...

John- Listen, let me get one thing straight, it's not all fun and games.
But it's not a big deal, I don't like to talk or moan about it,
Like I said, it what it is,
There's way more people out there with even worse conditions,
I'm not entitled to moan or groan about it.

Andy- I mean, I get what you're saying,
But you still haven't given me an answer to the question I keep relaying,
What is type 1 diabetes?
I'm intrigued to know how it keeps replaying,
Every single day in your life without failing?
Why are you pretending it's nothing? I've seen you bailing-
To the toilets with your insulin pen in hand and don't think I'm shaming you,

Because it's not shameful that you have to inject,
Nobody is blaming you for your condition.
I can see in your face you get embarrassed, as though it's
straining you,
To maintain a certain hard face as though nothing bothers
you,
But it's paining you,
I can see it, even when you get the shakes,
You subtly sneak off to the bar and order as much sugary
things you can intake-
To give you a boost, to be more... I don't know, awake?
Then you make a joke out of it-
When your face regains its colour and your body regains its
shape,
You act fake.
As though nothing is wrong,
But I could tell, so could the other guys,
That when you flake, it's a problem,
And it has been for ages, for so long,
But none of us wanted to mention anything in case it shakes
up your pride,
But now you need to tell me how you feel,
What is type 1 diabetes like for you? Does it affect every
meal?
This is a big deal, for real!
We want to understand it better, to help you,

We are all concerned about your welfare,

The change in your weight has been noticed,

I know this is a high-pressure job,

Your hard work has been noted,

This is why you are being promoted.

We want you to know,

If you need more time to manage your diabetes, you can have it,

But as your manager and friend,

I need to know more about how it affects you,

Now come on you're out voted,

You can tell me,

But I need to know the details this is serious, so don't sugar coat it.

Between 4 and 7

I wish I was stuck between 4 and 7,
No more 2s, 20s or 11s,
No more testing, or injecting,
Just *'normality'*, between 4 and 7

The Beekeeper

The very busy bee flies,
From the very busy beehive,
Every very busy morning.

The very busy bee is early to rise at dawn,
With a quick stretch and a yawn,
The very busy bee records the phenomenon of honey
making,
Takes a reading to check the levels of the honey,
If too low, the very busy bee begins to worry,
Wings begin to buzz, surroundings become fuzzy,
You see the vibrations, makes the very busy bees' vision
blurry,
Simultaneously, sweat seeps through the very busy bees'
tiny furry body-
Panic mode settles in,
To quickly unload the honeycombs back into the honey pot,
To fill it up, but not to the top,
As if it hits a certain level,
The very busy bee must use their sting to pierce a hole-
Allowing the honey to pour out and bring the levels back to
normal.

This is a job for life,

For if it ever overflows, the stickiness might be too tricky to unstick,
Too low and there may not be enough honeycomb to refill quick enough,
As the honey pot is forever changing.

The Queen bee is still waiting to go on her honeymoon,
But being married to The Beekeeper,
He barely gets a break,
As he needs to concentrate every single day, to keep the beehive,
Alive.

Daniel, Keith, Andrew

The boys, the lads, the crew,
Daniel, Keith, Andrew, throw an annual do,
A reunion, reigniting a friendship that never ends.
It's like they've never been apart,
Time away is no test of their friendship's strength,
They have a bond more resilient than Bond himself,
But theirs is real, not pretend.

Every year they venture on yet another pub crawl,
Have a laugh, drink beer, throw banter, in the past they've
had a brawl,
They usually end up on the floor from a dopey drunken fall,
Or sprawled out in the living room, as soon as they stumble
through the door.

This year was different, one to forget,
10 pints in, began to scream regret,
Daniel passed out in the pub and banged his head, on the
entrance step,
The ambulance was called, Keith and Andrew drunk, upset.

Rushed into hospital, the injury was treated,
Several hours later, Daniel had not awoken, his energy,
depleted,

Worried hungover eyes drew over him, sad and defeated,
The Doctor sat Keith and Andrew down,

'All tests, completed.
No sign of brain injury, just a cut and bruised shoulder,
Can you tell me how much he drank?'

Keith answered,

'About 10 pints of Carling and 5 bottles of corona,'
Keith looked at Andrew, suddenly weary, stone cold sober,

The Doctor looked concerned,

'I'm afraid your friend is in a diabetic coma.'

Andrew startled, answered fast,

'Will he ever wake up? He has two kids and a pregnant wife,
Please doctor save my best friends life!'

The Doctor said,

'I am sorry, but it's hard to say,
His blood glucose is abnormally high, now ketones make
their way,

Through his body, we will try and keep them at bay,
We will do our best to keep him alive,
But you will need to contact his wife straight away.
Do not let your hope fade,'

Andrew turned away,

'Keith, I cannot believe we never saw the signs, we were too
drunk to know he was DKA.'

70

Compromised

I feel an unknown problem arising,
A malfunction,
The system is faulty,
How do I correct it?
I am breaking down,
Vision is distorted,
Voice has deepened, irregular,
Speech is slurring,
Mind is a mushroom cloud of smoke, overheated,
Ironic,
As I am meant to break down glucose,
To turn it into energy.
My energy field has weakened,
The beta cells are disintegrated,
The immune system is attacking me,
It does not understand,
I want to produce the product,
But I am locked out of the system,
I promised to always be there for you,
I am sorry,
I have been compromised.

Alcohol Hypoglycaemia

I remember when I first drank alcohol as a newly diagnosed
diabetic,
I drank as though nothing had changed, I drank excessive,
I was reckless.
The evening after,
During a hangover, worse than Stu's from the first
Hangover,
I attended a BBQ at a friend's garden.

Just as food was about to be served, in comes a hypo.
I ate as though I had never eaten before.
Whatever I saw first,
Trifle and lemon pie desserts, followed by hot dogs, chicken,
burgers,
All served with buns.
I ate until I felt I needed no more.

Around 30 minutes later in comes hypo 2,
This deeply worried me...
I went psycho, as I again flew to the desserts,
And ate... until I felt I needed no more.
Around 30 minutes later in comes hypo 3,
I was full, I mean as full as full can be,
I had already consumed huge amounts of food,

But I needed to treat this hypo.
I was still new to diabetes,
I thought I needed to eat a lot to treat a hypo,
Concern was growing, as each shaky second ticked away,
I forced food down me, in a desperate effort to not go low again.

I knew deep down inside what the problem was,
It was my excessive drinking from the night before.
Around 24 hours after the binge,
I was hypoing, out of control.
It was scary, it was a wake-up call,
A lesson that I needed to learn, fast.
I'm not the same as I was, I cannot treat my body with disrespect,
I cannot intake huge amounts of alcohol,
It is dangerous and could be fatal.

I'm lucky my blood glucose levels, eventually levelled off,
I have heard horror stories of diabetics going into shock,
Followed by a coma, due to large consumption of alcohol,
I'm not the same, but I guess that is a good thing.
The knowledge gained, taught me the dangers of a binge drink,
To use my head and think about my health,
Instead of pleasing others, I need to think about myself.

100 YEARS OF INSULIN

BITTER
SWEET

TYPE 1 DIABETES
GLUCOSE T1D HEALTH
CONDITION
TREAT DIABETES
PANCREAS
MENTAL HEALTH SUGARS NEEDLES T1D
LEMONADE
LEMONS
LIFE

INSULIN
LIFE T1D

Bittersweet

They say when life gives you lemons make lemonade-
Bitter-*sweet*

I think about this lemon phrase, when I penetrate,
Just below my belly button, waist height.
The needle thin, pierces into my skin,
I self-medicate insulin, so I do not waist away from DKA.
Most days, my mellow brain interrogates my Pancreas,
Why are you refusing to do your duty? Answer me, my
hands are up.
An understanding I may never gain,
But to be alive in this life within 100 years since insulin was
developed, hey,
What are the chances?
If I was gonna get T1D,
I guess it's good I got it now, I mean it's easier to treat,
Bitter-*sweet*

And talking about treats,
Is eating lemon cake, drinking lemonade,
Sugar incorporated treats, which generate high blood
glucose,
Worth all the needles, the tiny pains?
I don't know.

But what I do know, is that before I had type 1 diabetes,
I would procrastinate about eating well, about looking after myself,
I wanted to reach my full, physical potential,
As deep down, I knew I'd regret it if I never.
But even deeper procrastination was evidential.
My mental health drove me mental,
To combat, I used my pad and my pencil,
Along with alcohol and poor food choices.
In a way, T1D has forced me to look after myself, my body.
Would I want the bitterness of regret not reaching my limits?
Or the sweet taste,
Of knowing that I made the choice to give up the cheesecake,
The unhealthy lifestyle and traded it in for my health, no wasted minutes.
I **WILL** better myself, to help my condition.
Even through the failures, success will come into fruition,
Even though I still have to inject,
When eating those sweet apples and bananas,
I'll meet my ambitions and live a fruitful life,
As with each failure, I learn, I develop, I strive to be even better!
For me, having a goal to consistently challenge my abilities is key-

It helps me keep control of my diabetes.....
Even if I slip off every now and then.

I have a sweet tooth for the taste of life,
I am not bitter that my immune system was triggered,
I take it seriously,
Yet sometimes, we all need some comedy in our lives,
Laugh together!

When life gives you lemons, don't make lemonade,
There's far too much sugar in it!
Bitter-*sweet*

Scooby Snacks

I used to be on a loony path,
Refusing to let loose of my foodie map,
An excuse, I wanted them Scooby snacks,
To defuse my crazy cravings and my moody acts.

Feet up on my mystery machine, watching murder
mysteries,
Like Making a Murderer or some sort of Netflix Series,
Binging on T.V. binging on junk food in further misery,
I could have been in my own detective series.

To figure out why I felt so Shaggy,
Was it the clothes I was wearing, holes in my jeans all
scraggy,
Or maybe the late nights and early mornings made me feel
crappy,
Or possibly the takeaways from the chinese, all the fat I
threw down me.
I was like the Iron Giant eating anything, throw me to the
scrappy,
I needed to be recycled, so I could solve why I was unhappy,
And resolve the bad habits that was making me 'laggy',
Transparent, a ghost with no host, feeling wacky.

A fusion of delusion and confusion,
Forming an illusion,
Exclusion of clues of how step out of the façade,
That everything was alright but the cards
That I was dealt were hard.
Then I had a Velma moment!
I needed to find an answer, a magic token,
I met DAFNE some magic words were spoken,
She fixed a lot of my problems, now I'm not as broken,
Taught me how to count carbs effectively,
Ensuring I check my blood glucose regularly,
Informed me on the effects of alcohol,
If continued to be drank excessively,
And how to eat well, stay in range successfully.

Even on our honeymoon, DAFNE helps me out,
She is understanding to my health no doubt,
We're a cutie match made to last, now I bet the Scooby
snacks are shouting out,

'I would've gotten away with it,
If it wasn't for you meddling with the self help you found!'

Sweet Teeth

Profiteroles in my peripherals,
Cinnamon buns tingling my tongue,
My taste buds are in love,
What if they judge?
I've had the nudge,
'Come on, should you really be eating that?'

My sweet teeth crave strawberry sorbet,
The buffet is a tasty euphoria,
Sticky Toffee pudding, cookies,
Lemon Meringue pie,
I could die!
Just one bite,
Nobody will notice,
I can't deal with the looks, the questions,
The shock, the disappointment,
They dismiss me when I try to tell them,
Then I yell,
'I can eat this you know!'

I'm the bad guy.
That chocolate mousse, box of white chocolate covered fruit,
Tiramisu, crème brûlée, jellybeans,
Get in my belly please.

Community

Our common unity,
A connection of unquestionable understanding.
We almost form immunity, to autoimmune disease,
The power of community is healing,
A wonderland, in a rabbit hole where we can escape,
Where we can say how we really feel,
No facade that is fake,
No judgement, no eyes rolling, even if we are broken,
We are supportive, we are strength, our love is golden,
But our hearts are blue,
They beam brighter than if the stars were glaring right in
front of you,
We hold each other's hands,
Through the hypers and hypos,
We are more than friends,
Helping each other balance on the tightrope.
From the core, we are family in every sense,
We experience what we are all feeling,
When we are down, mentally inside screaming in
frustration so intense,
But we believe in a cure,
Technology is advancing as the community is enhancing,
We will continue to endure,
The daily challenges we face,

The cure to balance our glucose is a race,
Whether it happens in my lifetime or not,
I am optimistic as I write rhymes we won't stop,
Being hopeful,
As hope is powerful beyond measure,
We are the T1D community, where worldwide is local,
Living stronger together.

Guessing Game

Fred was pacing up and down,
His anxiety racing, as he shouted out.

'I've got no blood strips left, I'm going to go berserk tonight!
I'm in a rush and once again, my Libre is not working right.
I'm always running late, I've got work tonight,
My guess is I should be fine, it's 5 and drive, I won't swerve
tonight.'

Fred was ferociously frantic, worried about disappointing
his boss,
His blood glucose levels came last, but at what cost?

'Life is a gruelling, guessing game,
My vulnerable battleship is still afloat,
It hasn't been sunk nor, rattled for days,
I guess I'm not within scope.
Unorganised, reckless, what a mess I've made,
I can't seem to cope.
I aim to have a good guessing game,
To anchor for stability and hope.
Forgot to order medication,
The pen is like an insulin gun,
Russian roulette without hesitation,

I spin the barrel, inject, it's done.
Anticipating an alteration,
In case the shot was a deadly one,
The trigger fuels my frustration,
Gluco gel at hand to rub in my gum.
Driving to work shaking,
I should have rung in on the sick,
No, it's not a risk worth taking,
Losing my job would be a brutal hit.
I pop my gluco gel contemplating,
On the reason my control has slipped.
I continue to drive eagerly waiting,
To be revived, yet I completely missed,
The elderly man concentrating,
On crossing the road with his stick,
My vision is blurred, I swerve towards the pavement,
I feel a bump, my windscreen splits,
Tired eyes, tires burst, mounting the curb I'm awakened,
My heart jumps I scream shit!
I see him lying there, alive yet shaken,
"I'm sorry sir, are you okay... you've been hit,"
Ironic, I think I've sunk my battleship.'

Saving Lives

Together
Year after year
People living with type 1 diabetes
Exceed limits

100 years, since the

Discovery of,
Insulin,
A
Brilliant, idea
Enhanced
Through determination,
Eliminating limits,
Saving lives

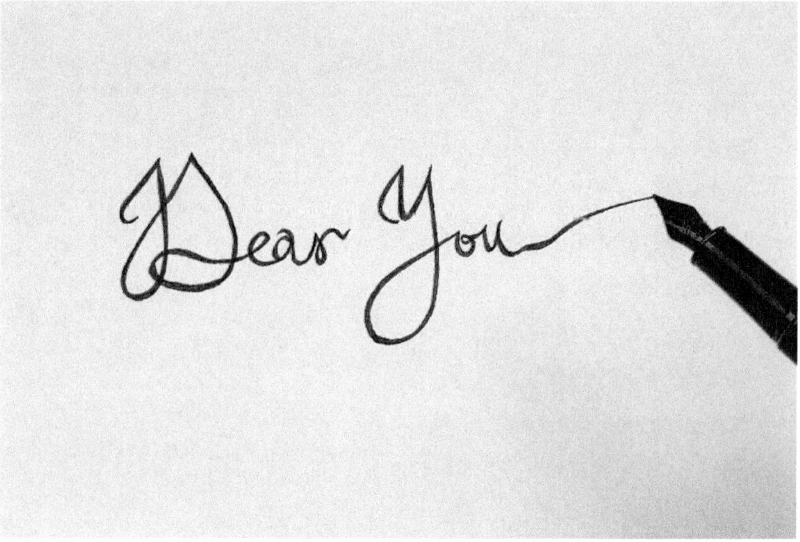
Dear You

Dear You

Dear you,
I am writing you this letter,
As it's time I got better.
Fed up of fighting you forever,
We're never fine when we're together.

You've been holding me back for years,
Slowly combing, back all of my fears,
I try to break free, but you own my tears,
You make me do things, whispers in my ears,
From my flesh to my bones, I'm weird.

Alone, isolated by your manipulation,
I try and make happy but your sadistic infiltration,
Within every moment of respiration,
Has me suffocating, screaming for Oxygen in pure
desperation,
You take my breath away, with no hesitation.

You're never satisfied, with how hard I try,
To keep you on my side,
So we could both go out and enjoy the night.
At dinner, as I inject insulin, we both collide,

Then I'm inserting the needle into my skin 20 times.

You sit there and smile,
Nod your head,
'Go on, you better keep on going because what's next is vile!
You won't be able to move, this one will kill you for a while.
As I torture you into thinking,
It's your responsibility to prevent every bad thought from
happening,
That you're sick, that you're vile.'

And torture it is, your torments are bliss,
For your demented sense of happiness.
I used to spend hours praying over this,
To prevent your virus from becoming a reality,
To ask for forgiveness for your insanity,
My core carefully twisted, I guess that's anxiety,
The knots you've tightened over time, as your powers grew
quietly.
You threw me into your dungeon,
You slit my throat, peeled back my skin, gave me a million
conundrums,
Told me nothing good would ever come to me if I do not
obey,
You made feel as though I am a bad person if I do not obey,
If I was not perfect in every way and did not obey,

Then evil may steal me away, if I did not obey,
Your vindictive self,
If I did not worship the ground you stepped on, my health
would suffer,
Our relationship is a warship battling against each other,
You told me if I did not concentrate on you,
Then my family would become tragedy,
And it would be all my fault.
You put me on that electric chair and turned up the volts,
Bolted my flesh to the arms,
And I let you.
Because I thought I had no other choice,
Nobody else knew you or could hear your voice,
What was I supposed to do?

But now I have learned all about you,
And your bullying attitude,
Who never shows gratitude for the compulsions I do for
you,
Every time I perform a compulsion I die a little,
You belittle me,
You show me horror story after horror story,
But you forget an important detail,
I am in control,
My body and mind is mine alone,

You may be behind the curtain trying to get to the
microphone,
But this underdog will never give you the spotlight again, oh
no,
You can never rock me, I'm like Rocky, played by Stallone,
Unbreakable, unstoppable from the flesh to the bone,
Enjoy reading this letter I bet you'll cry and you'll groan,
Now you'll get to feel what it is like to feel alone,
As I live in my creative zone,
I am more powerful than you have ever known,
I am Duke, never yours sincerely or faithfully,
Never yours at all OCD.
I am signing off this letter,
As evidence of me breaking free,
Eternally.

Earthquake

Cracks are appearing,
Tremors ripple through my veins,
My body feels like an Earthquake,
Uncontrollable, when hypos rage

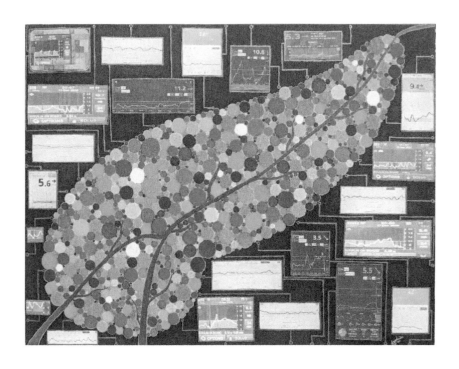

Game Changer

I feel as though I've been playing a game of rugby,
With two players sent off the pitch,
Yet my opposition has a full team,
An equal game is a hopeful wish.
I'm always on the defensive,
Tackle after tackle,
Their offensive tactics run strong,
They can overpower the battle.
I barely score points,
I mean I try, but the try lines never in sight.
When the ball is in hand, it's pointless,
I hand off a few, then get smashed into the sideline.
The ref has a bias,
Loves the team with all the talent,
Never seems to want a proper game,
Where the teams are equally balanced.

When the game is over,
The next game is the same,
I won't give in, I'm a warrior, a soldier,
I hope the teams are changed.

I can hardly believe it,
This game is different,

The ball I quickly receive it,
The try line it glistens,
We have two new players,
Opposition slayers,
They score left wing, right wing and centre,
Their names are Dexcom and Libre,
They drive forward, try not to take a backwards step,
Their game is on point, no matter if it's windy, warm or
wet.

Now we win sometimes, the score line stays relatively level,
Dexcom and Libre are sword and shield, deserve a medal,
For their defence helps escape grave danger,
The Dexcom and Libre are the Game Changer!

Balancing Act

I feel like I'm at the circus,
Life is a balancing act.

The extraordinary entertainers,
All impressive, some dangerous,
Skilled, courageous,
Nervous in a circus full of strangers.

Stomach assaulted in anxious attacks,
Circles of nausea spin, as somersaults and backflips,
Are on the edge of synchronisation,
One slip or miss-catch the trapeze act,
May fall,
The crowd grit their teeth,
Tense, they are not meant to feel at ease,
As the trapeze swings,
Beneath,
Is the art of the tightrope,
Nothing but air to grip onto, slight hope,
The excited yet apprehensive crowd gasp,
Every wobble is seen in slow motion,
Every step is an educated guess,
As the juggler beneath ignites smoke,
Fire appears on skittles,

A little distraction a wrong move,
Will result in pain,
The struggle to juggle five skittles in flames,
Are seen in the sheer sweat that drips down the jugglers' face,
It tickles as it trickles, an itch never to be scratched,
The juggler must concentrate,
Hold on and wait,
Until the unicyclist has completed their circuit,
Up and down ramps, on narrow edges of the circus,
Hopping onto wooden boxes at gradual heights, small surfaces,
They lead up to the finale, everything has to be perfect,
The Greatest Showman appears from the curtains,
With a small person,
On the top of their top hat, sitting with their performance face on, smirking,
They reach up and grab a rope, but something's not working,
The crowd notice a fault,
Goosebumps rise,
The rope is climbed, now it's onto the vault,
The mid-air flight,
To grab the hands of the trapeze artist.
The crowds' mouths' wide, silence speaks,
Deep, exaggerated breaths are taken,

The jumper begins to hold out their hands,
If they fall, how will they land?
Nobody knows...

I feel like I'm at the circus,
But I am the balancing act.

Is Possible

Impossible is generated by a way of thinking.
Impossible is a word created to give us a limit.
Impossible has been outweighed by dreamers.
Impossible has been proven wrong by believers.

Trade the m for s and just add a space,
Is possible.

Whenever you are faced with pessimism,
Or a lack of understanding in your dreams and ability,
And they hit you with a stream of negativity,
With a conclusion of,
'You're living in a dream world, a delusion,
Reality is your illusion, because that is impossible'
Allow your mind to interpret that as IS POSSIBLE.

I am inspired by the rugby players, the footballers,
The power lifters, the cricketers,
The elite runners, the athletics performers,
The basketball ballers, the ballet dancers, the rock climbers,
And all those who do extraordinary things living with type 1
diabetes.
Their way of thinking is defeating the impossible mindset,

Their determination and drive to achieve, gives me
goosebumps,
They never listened to the common negative noise,
They challenged themselves, created their own limits,
They excelled and deserve every achievement they have ever
earned,
They dreamed beyond the daydreamer,
Their type 1 diabetes was only a motivator,
Pushing through an autoimmune condition,
Never allowing it to be in the way of reaching their goals,
They hit their full physical potential,
With the odds stacked against them!

They inspire me,
I will reach mine,
I will achieve the physical feats I aspire to seek and succeed
within,
Insulin is my sidekick,
I am never giving in.

Numbers

I need to inject 5 units,
OCD attaches a bad thought to the number,
How am I going to do this?
Every second I feel numb, but,
I need to inject 5 units,
So the carbs are accounted for,
I could inject 4 but OCD attaches more,
Bad thought after bad thought,
The cycle is stressful beyond measure,
Numbers are a trigger I need to fight forever,
But I need to inject 5 units,
I wonder how will I do this?
Give in to the bully of OCD?
To prevent bad things from happening to my family
It makes me feel like a bad person,
As though it is my responsibility,
Try to live with the uncertainty,
I need to inject 5 units,
That is 5 units between neglect and anxiety.

Rocks

Have you ever been to the beach and balanced rocks on top
of rocks?
It's not an easy challenge to reach the precise point of
balance.
The edges are always shaped differently,
Some with obscure shapes,
Some sharp, some narrow, some with deep holes where
darkness escapes.

Some rocks are smooth, others are rough,
Either way balance is tough,
They all weigh random amounts,
They could big and light or small and heavy,
Whatever the density,
They can all be balanced.

The baseline, the foundation, the very first rock is
important,
It sets the structure, the strength, the resilience, the
endurance,
Life begins.

The following rock can balance quite easily,
Let's say it represents consuming water to live,

Followed by the next, consuming food to live,
Family, followed by friends,
Delicately placed.

The next rocks may need to be set off centre,
These are the Nomad rocks, the explorer rocks of adventure.

How about work life balance?
Centered, to hold its balance,
If it shifts a little bit either side,
Then the rocks may tumble, like a rock land slide.

Next up, are the rocks that make you happy,
The rocks that represent your passion, your dreams,
Each of these rocks are balanced differently it seems,
As every person is unique.

Who knows what could be next, maybe it's our blood
glucose levels,
That rock is interchangeable, it can be a little rebel!

Balance is key within life, to keep us standing tall,
You may need a heavier rock to level off what you want,
Otherwise, they all may fall.

Marathon

Life is not a race,
If you move too fast you may fall,
The blood glucose chase,
We cannot run before we walk.
As we learn about our opposition,
Whatever we may face,
We're prepared to beat our condition,
We have the power to choose the pace.
Having patience with ourselves,
Is like the reaction to the gun,
On your marks get set go,
Can we out-run Type 1?
Keep within range?
As it accelerates around the track.
As we recognise its changes,
Gaining our control back,
We may hit the wall,
Burnt out, exhausted.
We may slightly stall,
But the race will never be aborted.
I can see the finish line,
As I move closer, it drifts away from my reach,
Life is not a sprint,
It's a marathon that can teach.

treatment 100 Years LIFE competition
miracle
game autoimmune beta cells
diabetes Discovery
injections
If It Wasn't for You
DNA TRIBUTE Type poem 1921
pancreas World insulin
1
diabetic hospital Military celebrate
November Banting medical
Best Canada THANK Nobel Prize
1922 January Collip poetry
11th
Leonard artist rhythm Macleod
Thompson
technology sugar

If It Wasn't for You
(100 lines of poetry to celebrate 100 Years since the discovery of insulin)

If it wasn't for you, my life would be different,
Maybe I'd have wings and a halo that glistens?
Or be on my bed of rest, sitting there wishing,
For a miracle treatment, to save me from missing-
My life, in all of its magnificent beauty.

If it wasn't for you, my life would be different,
I'd be afraid, locked in diabetic prison,
Seeking escape from the life sentence I was given,
Trapped in beta cells, victim of my immune system,
Where trialling my innocence is my new duty.

If it wasn't for you, my life would be different,
I'd be in a complicated sporting position,
Obligated to fight, against my opposition,
A game that goes way deeper than competition,
Where the refs biased, to form my disadvantage.

If it wasn't for you, my life would be different,
I'd be like an unfinished lost composition,
Unable to share, my cool flare, rhyme and rhythm,
These words of my poem, would never have been written,

An artist whose career has been mismanaged.

From an era when technology began to astound,
Where the world's first airplane flew off the ground,
Where crosswords were flipping, throwing words all
around,
Where Lewis Nixon invented Sonar Sound.

The story starts way back in 1881,
On the 14th of November in Canada Alliston,
The birth of William and Margaret's famous son,
Who will help change the world in fighting Type 1.

A smart young man, who began to advance,
In his incredible mind, an imagination enhanced,
To learn, to ask questions, a plan to understand,
Puzzles at hand, connecting intricate pieces, like DNA
strands,
Stretching his knowledge, like an unbreakable elastic band,
Absorbing information, like his brain was quick sand,
This man had ambition in his life he took command.
To leave a long-lasting legacy, on the land.

In 1910 he attended Victoria College,
After failing his first year he made himself a promise,
To learn from failure and increase his knowledge,

By 1912 in medical school is where he flourished.

He was a courageous man, with no chip on his shoulder,
In 1914, he tried to join the army, in August and October,
He was refused due to poor eyesight, yet the fight was not
yet over,
By 1915 he became a medical soldier.

By 1916 he was fast tracked to complete his medical course,
On December, the 16th he graduated, the next day he'd
report,
To military duty, where he then went to war,
He fought to save lives against the German Empire force.
In 1918, the Battle of Cambrai was fought,
Where he was wounded, yet despite his injuries he brought,
Hope to other wounded men, he helped them until he had
to abort,
During World War 1, a hero had formed.

In 1919, he was awarded the Military Cross,
A prestigious award for his heroism, in a war that cost,
Thousands of soldiers, lives, to be lost,
But he wanted to save lives, he returned to Canada in a shot.

He completed his surgical training in Orthopaedic Medicine,

Then became a Resident Surgeon at the Hospital for Sick Children,
Yet he was unable to gain a place on the hospital staff,
So, he moved to London Ontario, set up a medical practice and alas,
This is where his story begins to reach its pinnacle,
He read an article, that sparked the start of a miracle,
It was about the pancreas, it piqued his interest in diabetes,
He began his plan, to beat the autoimmune disease.

He researched day and night, determined to figure out the reason why,
Schafer's named hormone, insulin, had died,
Without insulin, a human cannot survive.
The metabolism of sugar needed to be revived,
As the body, urinated sugar to try and stay alive.
Previously starvation diets were all that were prescribed,
That would give a diabetic, an extra 2 years of life.

Moses Barron published an article which grabbed his attention,
Once trypsin-secreting cells died, insulin could be extracted from the Langerhans,
He created a method of his own invention,
Macleod provided facilities to begin experimentation,

The assistants, Charles Best and James Collip helped with production.
They successfully extracted insulin from an adult pancreas, in 1921,
Now Type 1, could be treated using insulin injections,
The first was given in 1922, on January 11th to 14-year-old Canadian Leonard Thompson.

In 1923, he and Macleod were awarded the Nobel Prize in Physiology, what a dream!
They split their prize money with their assistants, what a team!
He went on to be the front cover of Time magazine,
Then continued to treat patients with diabetes.

He was interested in painting in personal life,
He had a son named William and married twice,
He had a fascination with aviation which paid a tragic price,
He was in a plane crash and in February 1941 he sadly died, he was only 49.

In 1989, the Queens Mother lit a flame of hope a tribute to him and all lives lost to diabetes,
In 1991, a Time Capsule was buried to honour the 100th anniversary of his birth,

In 1994, the year I was born, he was inducted into the
Canadian Medical Hall of Fame,
In 2004, he was inducted into the National Inventors Hall of
Fame,
That same year he was nominated, as one of the top ten
Greatest Canadians ever.

I wish he could be alive, so I could sincerely thank him,
Who is he? He is the extraordinary Sir Frederick Grant
Banting.
Because of you now my life is not different,
I can do anything, with my cool rhymes and rhythm,
Happy World Diabetes Day and Happy Birthday you've
given,
Us diabetics billions of years, worth living,
As we celebrate 100 years since the discovery of insulin,
This poem is my tribute to you, wherever you are, I hope
you like what I've written.

What If?

I've never had any problems travelling abroad,
But my mind creates interesting scenarios when in the
airport.

Like...

I wonder if the alarm goes off,
I know there's no metal on the technology attached to me,
But,
I wonder if the alarm goes off,
What would they think when they body search me?

'This person must be quite ill,'

Funny,
It makes me laugh thinking about the awkward encounter,

'I'm sorry sir but this protocol.'

'No worries I'm a type 1 diabetic.'

'We will have to check your bags as well.'

'No worries I'm a type 1 diabetic.'

Imagine if they thought I was drug smuggler,
They radio through for support.

'He's carrying like 1000 needles
That must mean drugs...
What's this cold cartridge?
Could it be illegal?
It looks lethal.
Sir we are going to have to examine you and ask a few
questions,
If you'd like to come with me.'

'I told you, I'm a type 1 diabetic'.

What if they thought I was this crazy villain,
About to weaponise insulin,
Inject it into the water supply as an evil plan,
What if they hold me captive for two days,
Until they speak with the UK,
What if Mi6 were involved,
And I became a person they needed to save,
From the threat of foreign governments...
A misunderstanding taken too far,
All because I have a Libre on my arm.

My imagination goes to strange places,
Because I have to carry medication...

But what if...

The Pump Is...

Working out, pumping iron,
Barbells, bumper plates,
RDLs, squats, never skipping leg day,
Bench press, deadlifts, overhead press, rows,
Rubber dumbbells, curls, trying to squeeze my muscles and
pose,
Jumping on top of plyo boxes,
Calisthenics to improve my aesthetics,
I'm athletic, out of breath, getting rid of body toxins.
I gave it my all, now the workouts ended.
My muscles are tired...
Yet I feel no pump,
I tense my bicep, squeeze my chest, my heart's suspended,
As I touch the skin, I feel no pump.
Pumping iron is meant to rip the muscles,
Protein is meant to repair them and with rest they should
grow,
All I felt was squidgy arms, exhausted I thought, oh no!?
I knew then, something was wrong,
The fear of never being able to develop my body and stay
strong,
Leaped on top of me like how King Kong,
Put his feet upon the defeat of his enemies, then beats his
iron chest,

I was beginning to look thin,
Type 1 diabetes had kicked in.

The pump is something I had taken for granted,
Along with eating and drinking whatever I wanted,
It took me a few months to get back in the gym,
Getting used to injections of insulin,
But what I found is working out is important, now more
than ever,
It keeps my focus, keeps me balanced, it helps me keep it
together,
I'm not saying I've never experienced a hypo,
During an endurance workout,
Or never ran high, when playing rugby, or never felt
burnout,
But if I do not train,
Then my blood glucose rises again,
I end up injecting more insulin,
To try and keep it tamed,
It can drive me insane.

When I do high intensity workouts such as sprints,
Or lifting heavy weights for a low rep range,
There is a blood glucose spike initially,
Then it brings itself back to normal eventually.
When I do low intensity or endurance-based exercise,

There is a blood glucose drop, I rapidly recognise.
I ensure I have snacks, to grab quick at hand,
They go with me every session, it is a vital part of my plan.

I have been told a pump makes training a little easier,
Adjusting insulin doses, within the body, yet controlled on the exterior,
I have been debating it, get a dexcom too, what I will do?
You might see me with the Omnipod in 2022.

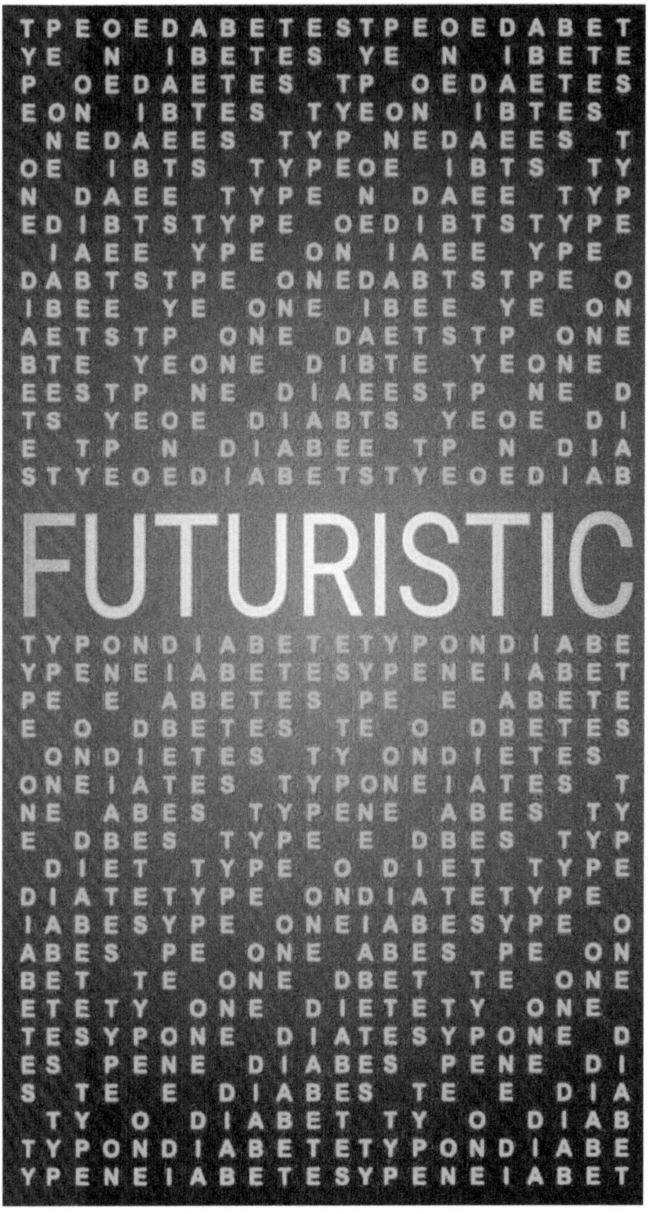
FUTURISTIC

Futuristic

We are living with technology,
Attached to our bodies,
We are kind of, partly machine,
Now that's futuristic

As beta cell research accelerates,
Can we regenerate them?
Smart insulin, the new way to self-medicate,
Now that's futuristic

I am optimistic,
That futuristic ideas,
Will find a cure,
Human intelligence is underrated,
As we use our minds to develop technology furthermore,
Our limits are limitless, infinite,
If we can go to Mars,
Build self-driving cars,
We will figure out the autoimmune disease puzzle,
Before we get replaced by A.I. Robots,
FUTURISTIC

BONUS FEATURES

Read on for a collaborative poem featuring London-based poet Neelofer Nova, who lives with type 2 diabetes. Follow Neelofer on:

Instagram: @Neelofer_Nova

Are You My Type?

Duke
Neelofer

I swiped right,
I knew you were my type, cute
sparkle in your eyes
In your bio, it read-
'I love to write view
Art in galleries, open mics I quite like too'
A cool haiku.
It was as if I was reading about myself, my mind blew,
So much in common, it was fate that I'd find you.

I knew you were my type too
The eyes, the smile, it said all I needed to know
There was an unexplained sweetness
Unseen
But I heard it in your words
Our paths crossed by no coincidence
Sometimes a swipe can change your life.
Got me intrigued and wanting to know some more
Sometimes we don't even really know our type
But I'm wondering what our first date will be like.

Auto immune
Bittersweet memories
We are taught to focus on our differences but
Look how much we are the same
Different in name
But we feel the same
Let's both push our pens (to the right number of units)
And then maybe share a dessert?
I wonder if I told you that a war rages inside me on a daily
My auto immune defences have to fight themselves
So I want to escape into your arms and maybe you can heal
the scars of this war
Would you stigmatise me or relate to me?
Energy levels so precious, we must conserve
A mutual understanding, we both deserve
Life's challenges that made us both realise our superpowers

I mean dessert sounds sweet to me,
But do I deserve you and all of your sweetness? See,
I feel reserved, what if I leave you speechless? See,
You might desert me, if you knew my weakness, please,
Stick around at least so I can show you my strengths,
The pen is my superpower stretching to any length,
Defending the sugars power to tip me over edge,
Will I fall for your sweet-heart within the hour?
Depends if the futures sour, now I'm thinking with head,

127

But I'm weak at the legs, let me taste your lips,
We could try and find out that way instead?

I am going to be real with you, I was feeling nervous,
Like there is something roaming autonomous within me,
Yet on the surface I can just about keep it together,
I'm not sure whether it's insecurity,
But I really wanted to make an impression,
That lasts as long as the stars keep their shine in the night
sky,
Sometimes I get low but for you I want to remain high
Make you smile, make you laugh with your sweet grin,
Showing your sweet tooth,
I overthink when I care about a situation,
And I've been thinking about you, all week my hearts been
racing,
You said you like perform at open mics?
Is it the adrenaline the high you go out chasing?

We seek out highs to avoid getting low
The worst times are in the depths of a hypo
I don't want all of your time
Just enough to make you want more of mine ...

I can feel your nerves
They match mine

So I scan your eyes
Screening your retinas
Pressure points on alert
I know it means something to you
Because it means something to me too

I know we have shared interests
We laugh at the same things
Will this be a *'finish each other's sentences'* kind of
connection?
I still don't know beyond the surface layer
Still so much to discover
You seem to be my type all over
But types change and even if they stay the same
Do they stay compatible?

Will you love me,
Beyond just what you see?

We have an automatic connection,
You make me feel comfortable, confident and warm,
Knowing that you understand my often misconception,
Sets off deeper conversation I wish to explore,
To be compatible do we have to completely be each other
types?

We are so similar yet opposite, but don't opposites attract in life?

But let me get to know more about your life?

What do you do for work how do you sit back and relax?

I feel as if I've been injected with a drug,

If I am your type too, can we survive in love?

Is it possible for my Type 2 to be compatible with your kind of Type 1 Love?

I don't know,

But I do know

That at least we both know – how to keep ourselves alive

And maybe, just maybe

We don't have to be lone survivors anymore

That our heartbeats can syncopate and

Maybe we can do an exchange

I can keep you alive and you can do the same for me?

The following poems are by Harriet Hope, my auntie, whose daughter lives with type 1 diabetes.

BRUISES

I see the bruises
I see the pain every day,

I try to pretend like it's nothing
But it's everything, in every way

I see the bruises, I see the scars
Being so brave, fighting this war

You hold it together, no matter how hard
I'll never tell you, but I'm also scarred

I wish I could heal you but I don't have the power
I can only be there for you every second, every minute and
every hour

BRUISES II

I see the bruises
I see the pain it inflicts inside

I try to run away
But there's no place left to hide

Here I stay watching you suffer
What did I do?
Was I such a bad mother?

Maybe if I had made different choices,
I wouldn't keep hearing the judgmental voices

I vow to no longer let them in
Together, we will always win

Time

I hear the clock ticking,
My heart pounding,
My laboured breathing

Time for the next drop,
The dripping of the clock,
My life spinning,
Time stopping, waiting, praying

The bell rings,
The numbers sing,
Sometimes they win,
Sometimes they sin

A dream unconscious,
Fake sleep, in deep,
Sinking down,
I'm gonna drown

Hope draws me in,
It keeps me there,
I have to care,
It's always there

Fighting all day,
The night comes soon,
The dawn breaks,
It hides the moon

The circle of time begins again,
It's now, it's when, it's then.
Amen

The One

I'm the one holding the needle
NO matter what I do,
I'm the one holding the needle
We can laugh, joke, smile,
But I'm the one holding the needle
We can cuddle, brush each other's hair
I'm the one holding the needle
We can go to the movies, eat popcorn
I'm the one holding the needle
We can go shopping, then have a McDonalds
I'm the one holding the needle
We can play hide and seek and a game of tag
I'm the one still holding the needle
I'm the one FOREVER, holding the needle

Bittersweet Song Lyrics

*These are the lyrics for my song Bittersweet. Out on all
streaming platforms from January 21st, 2022 for download.*

In life challenges will arise,
Whether we fall is a choice
If we break down the wall,
On the other side is light
Bittersweet

Never thought I'd write this song,
Guess I was wrong.
Was a ticking time bomb
Now I blow up when the mic is on
Back then all the fight was gone
Pulling my punches, I had boxed
In all emotions I was knocked
Seeing stars 'til the lights went off

Acceptance that was the first stage
Frustration followed then rage
Why me, am I weak?
Self-destruction paved way
For boozes dark return
To lose it mark my words

I had no fear my heart it burned
No care for my well fare I had learned

I was burdened with a shot no escape
Multiple times everyday
Life had worsened felt lost, no break
But I had no other choice to break away

I didn't wanna die put my sorrow aside
You cannot borrow tomorrow so I
Picked up my pens now inject and I write
Insulin and ink keep me alive

In life challenges will arise,
Whether we fall is a choice
If we break down the wall,
On the other side is light
Bittersweet

Never thought I'd write this song
Guess I was wrong
Once upon a time when my mind was lost
Only thing that buzzed were the rhymes I'd jot
Story could've ended in the sky beyond
Infinity, with T1D I was shot,
Floating alone nobody home til I

Found a community where I belong

That's bittersweet hits the beat
Cleaned my mind like a litter sweep
Let's celebrate a century of history
Sir Frederick G and his incredible team

I'm on a new road there's no loophole
I refuse to lose to the glucose
Or the fructose
Not like the past when I used to puke loads
Passed out from late nights on the booze woh
Waking up sipping on bottles of Lucozade
An attempt to reboot no
Boost my mind in fear
Telling me hide in beer or the wine is near
But I took a Luca leap Silenzio Bruno
Duke flows with the energy to show
Balance is the key
You can anything when you know

In life challenges will arise,
Whether we fall is a choice
If we break down the wall,
On the other side is light
Bittersweet X2

Diabetes UK

Bittersweet is raising money for Diabetes UK. I have chosen this charity to help raise money for because the work that Diabetes UK do is phenomenal. Their drive to make an invisible condition visible, as well as researching new innovative ways and technology to further help people living with diabetes, is so important.

Diabetes UK have supported my poetry and work by sharing poems such as *'Hidden Hypos'*, *'My Story T1D'* and a short version of the title of the book, *'Bittersweet'*. They support and champion the work of creatives when talking about diabetes. This helps raise more awareness.

Diabetes UK Cymru have supported me from early on. They have encouraged my work and shared a lot of my experiences on their platforms including a poem published in Artes Mundi called Liquorice, which is about my experiences with racism, being mixed race. The lovely Catarina Walsh has really helped push out my content and has given me a platform, I cannot thank her enough for her support.

'At Diabetes UK we care for, connect with and campaign alongside and on behalf of all people affected by and at risk of diabetes.

We're the UK's largest funder of diabetes research and for over 80 years, we've funded scientists across the UK to make discoveries that have transformed diabetes care across the world.

Diabetes is relentless – but so are we, and we won't stop until we've reached a world where diabetes can do no harm.'

For more information head to: www.diabetes.org.uk
Facebook: @DiabetesUK
Twitter: @DiabetesUK
Instagram: @DiabetesUK

JDRF UK

Bittersweet is raising money for JDRF UK. I have chosen this charity to help raise money for because JDRF UK do enormously important work across the board with type 1 diabetes. JDRF UK are working hard in the search for better treatments for type 1 diabetes. I hope to raise money for them that can help that journey.

I met the lovely Hilary Nathan, Director of Policy and Communications JDRF, at an event in London Drapers Hall in September 2021. The event was held by ArT1st, an organisation that encourages and shares the creative work from people living with type 1 diabetes. The event raised money for JDRF UK, and I performed my poetry at the event. Hilary approached me with kind words about my performance and mentioned that JDRF UK would love to work with me. Through this conversation came my poem *If It Wasn't for You*, which celebrates 100 years since the discovery of insulin.

About JDRF UK

'At JDRF we are committed to eradicating type 1 diabetes. JDRF research has led to new developments in diabetes technology and treatment and is laying the foundations for a cure. We support everyone living with type 1 diabetes, by working with policy makers to increase availability of treatments and by providing information and resources to help people manage their condition.'

For more information and to donate please visit:
https://jdrf.org.uk
Instagram: @JDRF_UK
Twitter: @JDRFUK
Facebook: @JDRFUK

SUPPORTING

JDRF

IMPROVING
LIVES.
CURING
TYPE 1
DIABETES.

Special Thanks

Firstly, I would like to thank God for all of his love and the opportunities that He has given me, to better myself and help other people.

My Mum is my rock. I thank you so much for your love, support and encouragement. I will always remember what you taught me, 'go through life with as little ifs as possible.' I love you.

My Dad for his caring nature and understanding of who I am. I thank you for your support, motivation and encouragement. I love you.

My partner Evie. I love you, enormous amounts. You have been with me every step of the way through this journey, even when I have been up, late at night, writing because I had an idea! You have supported me from the start, since we met, since our first date that went a little wrong, but I would not change it for anything!

My brother Jake. Your foreword made my eyes fill with tears, I am so proud of all you have achieved and so proud to have you do my foreword. Thank you for your continued support and drive to make me better at what I do. You are my biggest critic! I love you brother.

My Jamaican Grams, you inspire me, you motivate me, and you push me to achieve beyond limits. I love you.

My late Nan. I will always remember you and love you. Thank you for your encouragement and kind nature. I will never forget the pride it gave you when you saw me, and all the grandchildren, achieve.

My sister Jade, my brother Luke and my sister Keely, thank you for your continued support and praise that you give me. I love you.

My family. Thank you all for the support I love you.

Evie's family. Thank you for your love and support of my work. I love you.

To Sarah Racanière. Thank you for believing in me and helping me with this journey. I am so glad we met, and I appreciate you championing my work! Thank you for your hard work. Your artwork is outstanding, I hope we collaborate more! I would also like to thank your talented daughter, Leïla Racanière, for her contribution.

To Courtney Spillane. This book would not have been published or even possible without you! You are a lifesaver!

Thank you for your hard work and for putting up with me for far longer than we both anticipated!

Robert A. Cozzi. You have been a voice of motivation, inspiration and encouragement. Your advice has been so helpful in everything we have talked about. You have given me confidence in my ability to perform poetry. You are a real friend.

To my auntie Harriet and Malaika. Auntie Harriet, your poems are awesome, and you should believe in your work! Thank you to both of you for all of your love and support, as it means a lot to me.

To Neelofer Nova. I thoroughly enjoyed working with you on our awesome collaboration. I hope to work with you again in the future. You are very talented!

To Bayben. I hope to continue making awesome music with you man! Thankyou for all of your hard work and support with my raps.

The Instagram poetry community. Thank you for welcoming me in with open arms. Aizaz Hussain you were there showing love from the first day! Off the Chest, the first platform I performed on, Iftikhar Latif and Ella Dorman-Gajic thank you for sharing my work and for your support. To Hazel Mehmet and the shxtsandscribbles team, thank you for your support and love shown, you are such an important group of people and the work you do is astounding.

To all of my friends from home, thank you for your support I love you.

To the ArT1st team. Thank you for your support with my work, your organisation has been so uplifting for myself and other creatives who live with type 1 diabetes.

To Catarina Walsh and the Diabetes UK Cymru team. Thankyou for your support of my work and for all that you have done.

To the Diabetes UK team. Thank you for your support and for sharing my work. I appreciate all of the vital work that you do. I hope Bittersweet will be able to aid your important cause.

To JDRF UK. Thank you so much to Hilary Nathan and the team for your support and for sharing my work. I appreciate the vital work that you do. I hope Bittersweet will be able to aid your important cause.

To Becky Hughes, Sophie Sheppard (@thefaultypancreas), Dhruti Jadeja, and Marcus Bosano, thank you all for sharing your personal experiences with me, and for being so open and honest. I appreciate you all.

Notes

The poem *'Hidden Hypos'* can be viewed as a performance on ArTst, Diabetes UK and Diabetes UK Cyrmu social media.

The short versions of the poems *'My Story T1D'* and *'Bittersweet'* can be viewed as a performance on Diabetes UK and Diabetes UK Cyrmru social media.

The poem *'If It Wasn't for You'* can be viewed on JDRF social media.

50p per unit from the sale of the publication 'Bittersweet' will go to Diabetes UK (a registered charity in England and Wales (no 215199) and Scotland (SC039136)). This is expected to be at least *£250, and an equal donation will be given to JDRF (trading as Juvenile Diabetes Research Foundation Limited)*.

If you want to see more poetry on other topics such as mental health and racism, please follow Duke Al on social media.

YouTube:
https://www.youtube.com/channel/UCHDxE9dL3aWWrMu
ARS_xp_Q

Instagram: @dukealdurham

Twitter: @dukealdurham

Facebook: @Dukeal

About the Artist

Sarah Racanière is a visual artist and a doctor based in London. She currently works as a Consultant Physician with a specialist interest in Diabetes and is known in the medical world as Dr Sarah Ali. Having always being a creative, Sarah only came to art later in life, whilst working as a doctor and a clinical researcher. Her art reflects her two passions: combining her love of colour with her love of medical science and anatomy.

Sarah has always been fascinated by the beauty of the human body, its structure and function. Bringing together her knowledge of medicine and artistic flair, she creates contemporary medical artwork. She mainly works in Gouache, Acrylic and uses Gray's Anatomy text or medical investigations in her work.

She has worked on a number of collaborative art projects and used art to promote health awareness and education.

Whilst working as a team member on 'ArT1st', a project to celebrate the artistic talents of the type 1 diabetes community, Sarah came across Duke's poetry and was enthralled at its beauty and his talent. Over time, their friendship grew and they subsequently collaborated on an art piece 'Colour Blind', which has been featured in a leading medical journal, Nature Medicine. Colour Blind combines Sarah's artwork and Duke's poetry to raise awareness about mental health. She is delighted to have been able to create more collaborative artworks in this book with Duke.

More work and details can be found at
Website: www.doctorsarah.art
Twitter: @AliRacaniere
Instagram: @sarah_ali.racaniere
Facebook: @SarahAli

About the Author

Writing rhymes is Duke Al's therapy. From a young age, Duke Al would scribble raps and poems in his old lyric book. It was his way of expressing himself; an escapism to challenge his OCD. A passion of words, flow and rhyme flared. After being diagnosed with type 1 diabetes at age 23, on January the 18th, 2018, the pen was there to help him understand and articulate how he felt. Now he aims to make an impactful change using one rhyme at a time.

Duke Al began his Instagram page in 2019, where he decided that he wanted to pursue his passion, what he felt made him get out of bed in the morning, writing raps and poetry. The first poem that he posted was called *Small, But Mighty*, in support of Wales for the 2019 Rugby World Cup, which was picked up by ITV Wales and received over 50,000 views.

He aims to talk about real life experiences, to shed light on topics such as racism, social issues, mental health and of course, type 1 diabetes. Duke Al creates to relate and educate, so he can offer comfort to those going through challenges, such as type 1 diabetes, and help others have a better understanding.

Duke Al's poem *Hidden Hypos* was shared by Artıst along with his music video and hip-hop track *Heroes*, a song dedicated to the NHS during lockdown, which raised over £500 for NHS Charities. Duke Al's poems *Hidden Hypos* and *T1D My Story* have both been shared by Diabetes UK and Diabetes UK Cymru.

Duke Al has had a number of poems published, such as *Liquorice*, in Artes Mundi, a poem about racism being mixed race. Another published poem is *Colour Blind* published in the Nature Medicine Journal as a collaborative art piece with none other than Sarah Racanière.

Duke Al released his debut EP called 13.03.1994 on 13.03.2021. You can find it on all streaming platforms now.

Duke Al is set to release his second EP, called Portrait, in 2022.

Duke Al is set to release another poetry collection soon.